T0158122

SNAPPY BUT
HAPPY

SNAPPY BUT HAPPY

REVISED EDITION

Lorna Murby

authorHOUSE®

AuthorHouse™
1663 Liberty Drive
Bloomington, IN 47403
www.authorhouse.com
Phone: 1-800-839-8640

© 2012 Lorna Murby. All rights reserved.

No part of this book may be reproduced, stored in a retrieval system, or transmitted by any means without the written permission of the author.

Published by AuthorHouse   02/24/2012

ISBN: 978-1-4678-8526-3 (sc)
ISBN: 978-1-4678-8527-0 (e)

Any people depicted in stock imagery provided by Thinkstock are models, and such images are being used for illustrative purposes only.
Certain stock imagery © Thinkstock.

This book is printed on acid-free paper.

Because of the dynamic nature of the Internet, any web addresses or links contained in this book may have changed since publication and may no longer be valid. The views expressed in this work are solely those of the author and do not necessarily reflect the views of the publisher, and the publisher hereby disclaims any responsibility for them.

Photographs courtesy of www.thestudio17.co.uk

I wish to dedicate this book to my mother Maureen and my father Roy with all my love Lorna xxxx.

Introduction

My name is Lorna Murby and I'm now 35. I was born and bred in Coalville Leicestershire in 1971, and before I tell my story let me take you to the year 1999 on December 22nd.

In the wee hours of that morning I gave an almighty push and out popped Lydia my daughter. She was 6lb 8oz when she was born. I thought deep in my mind that the birth would be difficult, the labour would be prolonged and painful. I even thought I might die giving birth. However the birth wasn't as difficult as I thought it would be, I had an epidural to take away the pain, of course I wasn't having any of that.

After Lydia had been born she was so quiet lying in her cot. I was trying to comprehend the thought of being a new mum. I thought things would get easier given time, but they didn't. Things just got more difficult for me.

During the first night in hospital, following the birth, it was all peaceful and quiet, however just as I was dropping off to sleep, I heard screams coming from Lydia's cot. I thought she's not mine, if I leave her long enough she'll shut up but she didn't

When I tried to breast-feed I couldn't quite get the hang of it. Just as I thought I was getting the hang of it, all this milk was oozing out everywhere, I remember letting out an almighty scream and my baby was removed from my breast. The doctors were baffled as to what had happened, they thought I'd gone crazy, so they sent me to a hospital for the mentally ill.

I thought I was a failure as a mum. I remember my first night in the new hospital, clear as a bell, everything was so quiet and peaceful, I thought I might even get a decent nights' sleep, however that was not to be, all of a sudden Lydia started to cry, I couldn't pick her up, I felt so lethargic, so empty, I had no emotion for my baby. The nurses tried to help me by motivating me to look after my baby but I couldn't bring myself to pick her up. I had to make up bottles for her feed, that was such a drag. I simply had no emotions and no caring attitude for my baby, I just couldn't cope. Neglecting my baby made me feel so lethargic and empty inside, however in an ironic way I did care for her.

I was diagnosed as having postnatal depression and because I couldn't cope, my baby was taken from me for my own protection, but I'd never harm her. After the baby had been taken from me the doctors closely monitored me to see how I'd react when the baby had gone to be with the father. I was really upset and went into a deep depression. I wanted my baby back but the doctors wouldn't allow it. I wouldn't do anything to harm her. I started to develop feelings for her. I often yearned for my baby whilst in the hospital. Whilst in the hospital, later on the doctors realised I'd been mis-diagnosed. I didn't have Postnatal Depression, I had Bipolar Disorder (manic depression) and this is where I tell my story.

Chapter 1

What Is Bipolar?.

When a person has been diagnosed with Bipolar Disorder (manic depression) it can knock you for six. Being Bipolar you have many highs and lows in your life. I especially remembered the highs in my life. It was like euphoria at times, like being on a drug. I was stuck in a mental ward, six months at a time. During this time I experienced feelings of loneliness and depression. I had moments of euphoria which made me feel quite powerful at times, so I was instantly put on medication to lower my moods.

I was put on a drug called Lithium which is a mood stabilizer which is especially designed for people with Bipolar. Lithium comes as two different salts: Lithium Carbonate and Lithium Ciltrate. You can take either one of these drugs as long as you stick to the same one. Someone who takes Lithium has to have regular blood tests so that the amount of Lithium is safe and effective. You should drink plenty of water throughout the day and salt levels should be balanced. Are there any side effects from taking Lithium?

Yes there are. If you don't drink enough fluids then you can experience a deep thirst, increased weight gain and tremors. I was on Lithium for quite some time, however I wasn't taking in enough fluids so I became toxic and had to come off Lithium. Lithium is only potentially harmful if taken for a long period of time or by not drinking enough water. It can affect the Thyroid gland and Kidneys if not careful.

Bipolar is a brain disorder and is different from normal ups and downs that people experience in life. This disorder moves like a pattern according to a person's mood. If after being diagnosed you prolong treatment then these mood swings can interfere with work/family relationships. With the right treatment and professional care a person with Bipolar can lead a normal and productive life. Moods can vary, from a depressed state of sadness to an elated state of happiness or creativity.

Bipolar can affect sleep patterns and can affect every day functioning. Depression and manic depression are similar but different. A person that experiences this can feel happy and sad at the same time. Someone who has this sort of depression can experience a lack of sleep, have thoughts of suicide and experience a lack of appetite.

Someone who is suffering from depression can get very emotional in a variety of ways. You can experience feelings of unhappiness, tearfulness for no apparent reason, losing interest in everyday things, not being able to enjoy things you used to enjoy, getting restless, feeling agitated, feelings of hopelessness, fatigued, losing self confidence and experiencing feelings of suicide. These feelings are quite common amongst Bipolar patients.

Someone who suffers from Bipolar cannot think clearly when making decisions in life and can find it hard to concentrate. I found this to be true. Depression can affect physical well-being. You can lose your appetite or put on weight. You can find it difficult in sleeping, you can also find it difficult in waking up earlier than normal, experience feelings of exhaustion, constipation and also going off sex. Depression can affect behaviour patterns as well such as not completing tasks one at a time or taking too much on. Depression can result in crying a lot or not being able to cry. Someone who is depressed avoids mixing with others and can sometimes find themselves' confined to being alone at home like a prisoner in solitary confinement. Bipolar Disorder can affect everyday life.

I remember being in hospital and putting on some music, singing and dancing to the melodies. I really have a passion for music. I have a very gifted voice and I still love singing especially to a karaoke. I remember the queues to dinner they were such a drag. I remember once trying to escape over the fence in the hospital garden, I just couldn't get my leg over, about two or three staff nurses came after me. When you suffer from a mental illness, you feel trapped, stuck in hospital, that's exactly how I felt. I hated hospitals but I also felt safe and secure in one, funny but a strange notion.

By the end of the six months, I was starting to feel better so they let me go home. Now my home life had changed dramatically, for a start when I was in hospital I was married, but when I came out of hospital I found out I was divorced from Lydia's father. This event was a real knock down to me. I was so low so depressed because my marriage had ended.

I managed to find myself now living in a one bedroom flat, it was in Newbold Verdon in Leicestershire. It was quiet but adequate. It had to be my home now for keeps, I hoped, however my hopes were soon dashed to pieces. My landlady needed the flat for her father. I was left with the dilemma of finding somewhere else to live. It was stressful, difficult and tiring. However thanks to getting my name down on the council housing association and thanks to our creator, I got my place in Coalville. I was delighted, over the moon and thankful that I had somewhere to live.

I remember when I didn't have Lydia, I used to cry myself to sleep at night. I didn't at this moment in time have an understanding husband to look after me. I was really depressed living alone.

I had another manic episode and was back in hospital again. Whilst I was in hospital, whilst I was recuperating and whilst my medication was being readjusted, all my friends moved all my things to my new home and unpacked everything and put them away for me for when I got out of hospital.

I was used to it now, in and out of hospital. It was like a drug to me. I couldn't get a balance in my life; with my medication constantly changing my body, it felt like a chain saw had cut me in two.

It wasn't long before I had been in my new home that I ended up in hospital again. Whilst there I was under a consultant who monitored my progress. I did have a few more episodes of mania whilst in the hospital

Once I was really down so I broke a lot of crockery and cut my arm several times. It made me feel good so I did it again. I got a deep satisfaction from it. Smashing a plate to the floor gave me power so I smashed another. However afterwards I realised it was wrong. I was treated for minor cuts. You would have thought the staff would be bothered about what I'd done but they weren't because they were used to it.

It was whilst I was in hospital that I met husband number two. I should never have re-married because being Bipolar it affects judgement. I wasn't in the right frame of mind. I got married to the wrong man for all the wrong reasons. By this time it was too late, the deed had been done.

Married life was good to begin with, I had found someone to love again.

However as time progressed things went from good to bad.

I was so ill mentally and suffered from physical exhaustion from not eating and I got dehydrated from not drinking. One day my husband saw me lying in bed so he went into the bathroom, filled up a bucket of cold water and threw it all over me. It's a wonder I didn't catch my death. However I didn't let this get me down.

I slowly started to recover my physical health by showering, eating and drinking. I was soon back in tip-top condition physically but mentally I was on a downward spiral., back to my favourite place the hospital. It became a part of me and this started to worry me a little.

My husbands' visits became less frequent and we gradually drifted apart. I found out he'd been living with someone else so I divorced him. After I stabilized in hospital I went home. It felt so strange walking in my own home again. I had to cook for myself again so I started to buy ready meals to put in the microwave. I was sad, depressed and alone again.

I yearned for happiness but attention didn't crave me. Throughout my life two things have kept me going. First my faith, I'm a great believer in what the bible teaches and second my daughter she is so beautiful. I really do love her and miss her when she is not with me. You see I missed out on the first few years of her life. It was so hard to bond with her at first. In fact there were times when I felt like a stranger to her.

I'd often feel empty inside and the loneliness started to kill me.

Moving forward to the year 2004 things started to have a positive effect. My tablets were working. I started to stabilize slowly. Sometimes I'd suffer a relapse if I got too high. I very often found this to be the case. Throughout 2004 my mood was manageable but I wasn't cured of Bipolar Disorder. In fact at present there is no known cure. I always coped the way I could. By 2005 I was learning to cope with the fact that I was now on my own, I had depression, manic episodes but happy. I have learnt that as the years pass me by, to count my blessings. I have a wonderful little girl who is so precious to me and of course not forgetting my friendship with God, he has helped me learn to cope with manic episodes.

He understands me better than I know myself. I really put myself in his hands, he moulds me, shapes me into something good.

The past few years have been kind to me although I've had my share of ups and downs. Although I try not to dwell on negative emotions, I try to dwell on the positives in life. It's not easy when you have anxiety and worries to feel good about yourself, but I try to look on the bright side of life.

Lydia my daughter has been the centre of my life. She has so much energy for a six year old, so much get up and go. Ever since I had Bipolar my C.P.N. (Community Practice Nurse) has supported me, giving me sound advice for my well-being.

Moving on to 2006, this year has been a good one, a few ups and downs, but nothing major to report. I have been out of hospital for at least 2 years now. I still like to keep busy doing things to keep me occupied, keeping active prevents me from relapse.

My life is so much better now. I am positive in my attitude toward life in general, my mood swings have lowered dramatically. I am in a calmer more stable mood now, more than I've ever been in my life. I feel at peace with my inner self. I am more creative, industrious and out-going. I feel I can do absolutely anything to make life more bearable.

Bipolar isn't an easy condition, but one you can learn to live with. You need to feel in control. There are many times when I nearly lost my mind but thankfully prayer has helped me to regain strength and renew my vigour, to serve our creator to the best of my ability.

Bipolar patients need to feel loved and wanted by their family and friends. Many people don't comprehend what a Bipolar patient goes through; it can be mentally disturbing at times, thoughts running round your head and many sleepless nights. When someone in your family suffers from Bipolar, it can be very distressing for other family members. It is good for family members to find out as much as they can about their family member who is suffering from Bipolar as this will help them be more understanding and compassionate. Sometimes someone you love may experience suicidal feelings. If this is the case with you seek professional help immediately from a supportive organization. A person with Bipolar needs constant support from their family. You need to work with family members to agree on a course of treatment that is best for you. If worse things come to the worse, then a person might need to be hospitalised if they are found to be at risk to themselves or at harm to others.

Some people may wonder what triggers mental illness? Well it starts as a chemical imbalance in the brain, which affects the brains ability to function properly.

Going back in time once more I remember vividly having been talked into E.C.T or (electro convulsive therapy). What is E.C.T? E.C.T is a treatment given under a general anaesthetic, and is also used for severe depression which involves passing an electrical current through the brain in order to cause a fit. It's often used for severe mania as well. This treatment can cause a person to experience severe or slight memory loss. I experienced severe memory loss as a result from the treatment.

I have a job remembering things at times. I have learnt to live with the illness so to speak, to fall with the punches. The hospital staff tried to reassure me that this treatment would lift my mood swings, however I started to experience severe memory loss as a result of the treatment. Life is indeed a precious gift from God. When you think about it we were created with the ability to choose our path in life, to make our own decisions in life.

Life is to be enjoyed with your loved ones. I believe that humans have the ability to cure some illnesses themselves. We have so many pills to make us better but unfortunately there is no present cure for Bipolar. Maybe in time there will be a cure. Sometimes it takes a lot of stamina to keep well. I must say for me life is sweet and dandy. I am currently in remission and doing really well. I am ok as long as I keep taking my tablets.

I now focus on the body God gave me, showing respect for self and the determination to carry on regardless. If I have a bad day I don't fret about it. I just take it in my stride. I am so well now I have started to feel good about myself whereas before when I was really ill I couldn't do all the things that I wanted to. I remember once when I had a manic episode I behaved rather inappropriately by running outside with no shoes on, it felt exhilarating and fun. It felt so good running down the street in broad daylight with no shoes on my feet. I had a few people stare at me but I didn't care, I was happy but manic. Since that period in my life, mania hasn't been a problem in my life. I have settled down, I'm more at peace. I am used to being on my own and maybe I'll stay on my own for a while, anyway I'm getting used to my own company, the new me. I am more out-going and I have a good insight to the future.

Although I am in re-mission I still sometimes have bad days. Bipolar is actually a disease, a chemical imbalance in the brains' chemistry to function properly. This sort of illness doesn't disappear like a headache does. You have to learn to live with it, it's a fact of nature. I am learning to cope with Bipolar. I try to take my mind off the illness by keeping busy. One way I keep busy is by helping people with their troubles and worries. I try to reason with people from the bible, especially to people with medical problems, that there is an answer to all the problems we face in life. The answer is Gods' kingdom, which is a government that will rule over the earth. All Christians pray for this kingdom to come in their everyday prayers. Gods' government (kingdom) will abolish all mental illnesses and also all other illnesses forever and no one will say I am sick. I can honestly say that now is a good time to reflect on life and to see the good that's come out of it. Do you know what has kept me going for the past year? Firstly my faith, I'm a great believer in God. You can talk to him at any time, day or night. He is a good listener and can help you through any problem. Secondly my daughter is a good companion and a raison d'etre for myself.

The recipe for life is to have a positive mental attitude. It is not easy to do this but if you adopt this attitude you can experience positive results. I am now moving on in time to relate an experience from a friend who suffers from Bipolar Disorder. My friend lives in Scotland. I will now relate her story.

Chapter 2

Isabels Story

My friend is 63yrs old. She was born and bred in Calternix in Scotland. She was born in 1943 and has suffered from Bipolar Disorder for 26yrs. She was first diagnosed with the illness in 1982. It took doctors long enough to diagnose her. In fact she spent she long periods of time stuck in hospital, in a mental ward full of other Bipolar patients.

Before my friend got sick she was the picture of health, quite well in herself. In fact she was a woman with her whole life ahead of her. My friend became ill at the young age of 35yrs old. She was supposed to be at the prime of her life. After a long painstaking ordeal my friend was finally diagnosed with Bipolar Disorder (manic depression). It took 4yrs before she was properly diagnosed as having Bipolar. My friend was in and out of hospital. Before she was diagnosed the doctors didn't know what was wrong with her neither did the police. My friend was in and out of hospital for at least 10yrs. My friend was on a lot of medication, like myself, she started to stabilize and feel normal again. Whilst in hospital she felt safe and secure, like myself. She felt like no one would harm her. It was like being protected in bubble-wrap in a protected zone.

In order to control her mood swings my friend was instantly put on medication. She was up one day down the next, a bit like a roller coaster. Although my friend was ill she often found water to be relaxing, therapeutic, so soothing and tranquil.

When she was out of hospital she went to Tenerife quite frequently for a holiday and this made her feel much better. It has been said that a good holiday does you the world of good.

She has a very supportive family. They helped her during the good times and the bad times. My friend has five sisters and they are a close-knit family who helped her during her ordeal. This went on for 26yrs. When my friend was ill she depended on the love and support of her family. However many people don't understand a person who is manic. In fact some people tend to stay away from Bipolar people because they think you can catch it, well you can't. Bipolar is a mental condition not a physical one. You can get high or low moments in your life. You can experience moments of high energy. Many family members don't understand how a Bipolar person feels. Some people think Bipolar is contagious. It can be hereditable but in my case it wasn't.

Bipolar patients suffer moments of Euphoria. In fact you can feel like a super-woman or a super-man who feels that they can do absolutely anything. Like my friend I have experienced racing thoughts and a considerable amount of a lack of sleep.

Millions of people suffer from sort of depression in their life-time. Some times someone who is depressed can have a tormented mind. Like me and my friend millions world-wide suffer from some sort of depression in their lives. It is staggering to know at least over 330 million people world wide suffer from depression. Sometimes the torment is living with the disorder. Some people suffer with S.A.D or (seasonal affective disorder) which only occurs during certain seasons of the year.

What are the major symptoms of depression?

Major symptoms of depression:

1) If you think you have depression there are certain symptoms you need to look out for. Some one who is depressed can be like this for a few days or for weeks at a time.

2) You can lose the ability to do pleasurable things like you used to do before you got sick. Nothing is appealing anymore. You can loose interest in normal day to day activities.

3) A Bipolar person can suffer either weight gain or weight loss.

4) You can experience extreme fatigue or insomnia.

5) Motor skills can either speed up or slow down.

6) Many Bipolar patients are troubled by excessive fatigue syndrome.

7) Another major symptom of depression is having feelings of worthlessness and having negative emotions about yourself.

8) Another symptom of depression is a loss of concentration. I often found this to be the case and so did my friend.

9) A sufferer from depression can be so wrapped up emotionally that they find there are no answers to problems and resort to suicide.

This is one of the things that pained me. I used to feel like this but now I'm well. It was the medication that stabilized me and also my friend as well. Both me and my friend would agree you have to live with a mood disorder. So as I said before, it becomes a part of you and to be completely honest I would be lost without it.

Bipolar seems to effect not only women but men and children too. When depression strikes, it's as though it can burn a hole in your pocket. Depression can shake you to the ground with no way out as it may seem to the sufferer. It can affect someone's whole life. It can be debilitating and as some people may think, it can shake you to the core, with no end in sight.

Manic depression can cause the sufferer to experience uncontrollable bouts of weeping, sometimes profusely and for no reason whatsoever.

For a lot of people who suffer from depression, there are frequent moments of intense sadness.

When there is a person in your family who is suffering from depression. It can overwhelm the rest of the family because they care for you and they want you to have the very best for your well being.

When you have children they can often detect when a parent is unwell (as do animals). For some strange reason children tend to know. It is also noted that Bipolar patients can become snappy or angry easily. Like myself, my friend found that she had lots of energy, a bit like a super-woman. This is not uncommon. I often found that some people would avoid me because I was manic.

However now I'm well I find people want to be around me and this makes me feel good about myself.

Bipolar is a chemical imbalance in the brain. It is not contagious. I found when I was ill there were moments when I couldn't get out of bed. In fact I was bed ridden for a while. I didn't eat, rarely drank and I didn't wash for a while. It was only when I was prompted to look after myself that things slowly reversed. It was only when

I started eating, drinking and washing, that I got stronger, I began to function properly. I gradually got better.

Both mine and my friends' lives have changed dramatically for the better. She is only on two tablets a day. She is an extraordinary woman, full of confidence and poise. She really inspires me to carry on. My friend recommends that you take your medication as prescribed. Taking medication isn't a sign that you are weak but it's a sign that you are strong willed and have the will power and stamina to succeed in your plot against this monster of an illness.

I find the bible very comforting and soothing, a strengthening aid to my recovery. I also find the bible an anchor for the soul. Prayer is very faith strengthening. Sometimes people who are Bipolar need space on their own, other times they need to be surrounded by family and friends. If some one is going to aid a sufferer they need to show a sympathetic attitude. The last thing a person needs is to be told to snap out of it. A Bipolar person needs to be loved by family and friends. This is exactly how my friend felt; her family were so understanding and lovingly supported her during her illness.

My friend is going to relate how she was during her illness before she got well. So we move back in time to when my friend was manic. She has a frightening experience that she wishes to relate. My friend was very unwell.

She imagined she saw some one in her cellar wanting to shoot her. She locked herself in the house and the police had to break in to see if she was alright. When they saw her they knew something wasn't right. She was alright when the doctor arrived; he gave her an injection to calm her down, this lasted for three days.

In my manic episode I saw blood coming out of my veins, I remember running upstairs, screaming, getting in the shower to wash the blood away. I had another manic episode. When I looked through the kitchen window, I imagined I saw the devil. It frightened the living day lights out of me. The next day I went into town and bought some net curtains for my kitchen. I was scared of the dark after that.

Another experience from my friend was when she was in hospital, she was putting on make up on in her mirror when she imagined she saw a pig in the mirror looking back at her in the reflection. It was very comical. She also had another experience, she looked into the mirror and thought she saw Jesus dying.

My friends' depression was more intense than mine. My friend suffered for 26yrs of her life, which is a long time to endure the pain and suffering depression can bring. My friend has one more episode of mania to relate:

My friend imagined she was on television and the people were talking to her, having a conversation with her but of course it wasn't true but to my friend it felt so real like all the other experiences she had. My friend has had so many traumas in her life; it's unbelievable, suffering so much anguish and pain. She has suffered so much in life, yet she has come through it all.

I can relate another experience Something happened to my friend in hospital. She wanted to pick up a chair and throw it through the window. It happened to be Christmas day and she wanted to be with her sisters, instead she was stuck in hospital. She was irritable and snappy so she went to a shop, brought some alcohol and drank the lot. It made her feel more relaxed and calmness set in motion.

I'm not saying alcohol solves problems, of course it doesn't. It only makes the problem worse. The main help to overcoming depression is to have a stable family and lots of supporting friends' to support you when you are ill. They need to be kind and understanding to family members who suffer from Bipolar. Whilst my friend was ill her family looked after the house for her. Sometimes when I get in the mood, I run round like a head-less chicken spring cleaning and wearing myself out.

Another incident happened to my friend:

When my friend was at home she went out in the early hours of the morning at 4am posting letters. At this time of the morning anything could have happened to her.

My friends' recovery didn't happen over night. It happened gradually. Some people recover quicker than others. I'm still at the recuperating stage, not fully recovered yet but still battling on. My friend in Scotland is living proof that you can get over Bipolar. She displays a positive attitude towards life and this is how she survives.

In 1988 she was put on a powerful drug for 18yrs of her life and she hasn't been up or down since. She hasn't had any anti-depressants for her illness. Whilst she had been ill all her housework had been done for her. My friends' endurance and perseverance are to be commended. She had a tough life when she was unwell.

I hope you begin to realize how some one who suffers so much as my friend did, has come through it. She is an inspiration to me, a real tonic, minus the gin. She has proved to a certain degree that you can cure yourself; you need to develop a positive mental attitude towards life in general. To look at my friend now, compared to what she was back then, she's a new woman with a new lease of life. It is so amazing; she has such courage. She has proven to the medical authorities that it is possible to recover from a debilitating illness back to renewed strength and vigour. You wouldn't think that my friend was 63yrs old. She is so attractive and well groomed. She is so glad to be normal again. What is normality?

Well some one who is high or low feels at peace with their inner self, then that is what I call normal. My friend got the all clear from the hospital after over 18yrs of her life. She is to be admired by the outside world for displaying a positive mental attitude on her release from hospital. She was beginning to live life to the full.

Like my friend I have found inner peace within myself. I am more out-going and people want to be around me, whereas before when I was manic people moved away from me, they didn't understand me, and the way I was feeling. I think my friends' experience in life will inspire other readers to become well again too. A positive mental attitude is essential to life. Well that's my friends' story anyway.

It's very enlightening and sad in places but throughout all the trauma and mental anguish my friend has come through it all, as a better person, in more control of her life than she has ever been before. You see Bipolar, according to me and my friend can be overcome.

Just the other day I was in the local library and I said to some people "Do you know I've got Bipolar Disorder?" People smiled at me. "No we didn't know that, you don't look ill. "You look so well" said another person. I felt so good, on cloud nine again. I felt like an important person. We are all important and unique. Wouldn't life be boring if we were all the same, like robots. Anyway how does depression start? Well if you read chapter 3 you will find out.

Chapter 3

Practical Ways To Help A Sufferer

I can understand how people feel when they become depressed. I've been there too and so has my friend. When some one is depressed, they are up one minute and down the next, a bit like a roller coaster and believe me I've been on one and Bipolar is scarier than the fun fair. Writing from personal experiences has helped me tremendously. Before I got sick I used to hold down a full-time job and I was married. Here is some practical advice if you are depressed:

1) Seek a medical experts' advice immediately. Don't let the depression get worse. Your tablets are your life line; they are prescribed for your well-being.

2) Talk to a sympathetic friend or family member. It can be very soothing to the soul. It can elevate your mood

3) Be positive, look at things in a humorous way, see the funny side of life.

4) Put your favourite CD on and have a good sing, you'll feel much better and your mood will start to lift.

5) Take up a hobby or do something which you enjoy. I like writing, it gives me peace of mind.

6) Pray as prayer enhances your life. I have found this to be true.

There are practical points to bear in mind when suffering from depression, whether it's Bipolar, clinical or seasonal affective disorder. There is one major factor which sufferers need to be aware of: you can suffer from lack of sleep. I have found the bible to be soothing to the bones in time of need. I am writing this true to life story to inspire people not to give up in the fight against depression.

There are millions of people out there who suffer from depression. Both my friend and I have experienced depression. When you feel depressed you feel like you're in a hopeless state. No one in the world, not even doctors know what causes the disease. However what I do know is it affects changes in the brains' chemistry. A chemical imbalance in the brain can result from something that has happened in your lifetime. It could be a change in circumstances: i.e. divorce, family breakdown, or the birth of a child. In my case, after I had given birth to my daughter I experienced problems looking after her, no one is to blame, but sometimes I blame myself. The problem starts with a chemical imbalance in the brain.

I have read a leaflet somewhere about Bipolar Disorder entitled:

"An introduction to Bipolar Disorder". It has helped me to cope. The leaflet said that the average age of a person who suffers from Bipolar Disorder is in their mid 20s'. Bipolar patients need to be positive in their outlook in life.

Suffering from depression has helped me to discern what's wrong with me and to come to an amicable solution. I am fighting every day to conquer my illness; you need to do the same. Don't give up. Once you have conquered depression you can re-build your life again. I must admit that re-building your life isn't easy. If you gradually build stepping-stones, this will help you re-build your life.

Depression can be inflicted upon anyone at any age, this does include teenagers. It's a worldwide illness. It's important to get professional help, don't leave it too late. Most people feel better once medication kicks in. Remember to take your medication at all times, without your tablets the results could be disastrous to your mental health. A person who is mentally ill hasn't got his full mental faculties at the time of the illness. To recover completely from your illness you need to be positive, positive, positive. Take one step at a time, don't over do things otherwise you could become ill again.

Now me and my friend are well in ourselves, we both feel we have a new lease of life. Recovering from Bipolar doesn't happen over night. It takes a considerable amount of time for some people. My friend suffered for 26yrs of her life and for 18yrs of her life she has been well. So you see it is possible to recover, however you need will-power and determination to succeed. Whilst my friend was recuperating from her illness she learnt how to count her blessings in life. There are people in the world a lot worse off than we are.

Being in a mental ward is nothing to be ashamed of. From personal experience when I was in hospital, it was a harrowing experience, one I wish to forget. You can conquer your illness but it takes guts and determination accompanied by a positive mental attitude to life. People that suffer from mental illness can fully recover providing they get the medical advice they need.

The best advice I can give is: Don't isolate yourself from the outside world. Isolation can cause depression. You can experience feelings of worthlessness or loneliness. If you are to recover from your mental condition you need to train your mind to dwell on positive things rather than negative things.

When I had my pet cat Sooty, he was a tonic, he used to cuddle up to me on the settee, nice and snug. Pets can be used to help people in times of crisis. Sometimes some one who suffers from Bipolar feels that family members don't care and that they are a burden to their families.

I have stressed several times the importance of being positive as this can enhance the quality of your life. A depressed person doesn't always make the right decisions in life. Sometimes some one who is clinically depressed often feels that their whole life is in a fog and they can't find their way out.

When you are depressed you can lose your concentration. I found myself constantly forgetting things. I had poor concentration levels. I found myself like a spinning top going round and round, never stopping. During my illness I found that my moods had changed constantly from high to low. This is completely normal for a Bipolar sufferer.

The worst thing a depressed person can do is bottle up their feelings. You need to talk openly about how you feel to someone you are close to, someone with whom you can trust. Also you might find it useful phoning a friend, (but don't ask the audience or do 50 50). Phoning a friend always seemed to work for me. I'd often find myself on the telephone for an hour at a time. I wasn't that bothered that I'd run up a bill. Both me and my friend experienced the same symptoms: worthlessness, fatigue, disturbed sleep and blaming ourselves for our current condition. Some times someone who is depressed feels like they can't go on. Sadly some people have resorted to suicide. This believe me isn't the answer to your problems. If you experience any of these symptoms than seek professional help immediately.

Some people who experience depression suffer from panic attacks and have dizzy spells. This is the case with me. I sometimes feel the attacks have got much worse so I had to see my G.P who prescribed Propranolol which has helped me calm down. Bipolar people can seem loud or overactive in their thoughts. Some people feel that they are super human or even famous. I must admit for a while I did feel like super woman but now I'm back to normal. I am starting on the road to recovery. It's a slow recovery but can be attainable. However bad your condition you shouldn't blame yourself for your illness. It's a chemical imbalance in the brain.

STEPS ON THE ROAD TO RECOVERY

1) Recognise that you have a problem.

2) Seek medical advice for your well-being.

3) Remember to take your medication. It can reduce or stop your illness from recurring.

By taking your current medication, it can eventually put the balance back into your brain. If you continue to take medical advice and listen to your G.P or psychiatrist then there is a good chance you will recover from your illness. One way you can help yourself is by taking time out for oneself. Depression can affect every day life. It affects decisions in every day life. Depression affects a large majority of the worlds' population at some point in their lives. The only way to recovery is to some degree is to help yourself. You know the saying, a problem shared is a problem halved.

I am now going to relate how to combat your illness. It is extremely important that you continue to take your medication, as this will aid to your recovery. As I've said before you need a loving and understanding family to support you. In fact my family and friends have been very supportive to me. My faith has been an anchor for the soul, it has kept me afloat.

When some one is depressed they sometimes go off their food. Try adding fresh fruit and vegetables to your diet. When you are feeling low pick up the telephone and speak to a friend. If possible go and visit a friend for a chat, this will lift your spirits. You need to be strong willed if you are to be a success in life. I find listening to music lifts me up and motivates me to do things.

I try to be more active by keeping busy. I have lots of things on the go such as: crosswords, I'm a fanatic. I also enjoy knitting, writing, watching television, reading and making jewellery for fun. So what I suggest you do is take up a hobby, something which interests you. I find knitting very therapeutic. A hobby can fill the emptiness in your life.

When I was in hospital I found different activities very useful for the outside world. I made myself a cooked breakfast in hospital and this gave me confidence for when I went home. Also whilst I was in hospital I remember planting some Japenese onions in the hospital allotment, unfortunately I recovered so I never saw the onions grow. There was also a singing music group on a Friday. I always attended this group as I love singing. Everyone applauded me. This was my favourite group, I got really high on it. I also did a course on computers. I found keeping busy stopped me feeling depressed. I used to think alcohol would stop me feeling down but it didn't. You need to be strong willed if you are to be a success in life.

Chapter 4

Analysing The Symptoms Of Depression

For most of the general public depression is a part of every day life. You just have to learn to live with it the best way you can. Since I became depressed I put on a considerable amount of weight. Even though I'm over weight I am happy with in myself apart from my chest, I wish it was smaller. I feel much steadier and calmer in my moods now. I'm still trying to combat my insomnia; I still find to this day sleep difficult. I've started getting up earlier. One day I got up at 4.45am and started doing housework, by the end of the day I was shattered, however I went to bed feeling very exhausted from the days' activities. My whole body clock went out of sync. Now I get up at a reasonable time after 8am, this is a more reasonable time for me.

My friend is up and about at 7am each morning. She starts the morning off with a luxurious bubble bath as a treat. Next she has a good breakfast and then starts on her chores for the day. She's a very good example to follow.

I'm not yet in a routine, I'm just getting used to getting up earlier than usual. I'll have to work on the housework I'm afraid. Looking back in time, when I was depressed, I felt fatigued all the time, I had no energy. I often felt like this during manic periods of my life.

A lot of people who suffer from depression have recurring thoughts of suicide. Thankfully I don't feel like this anymore. I have so much to live for. I have the most beautiful daughter in the world, which is more than I could ever want. My daughter is like my best friend, we get on like a house on fire. When my daughter isn't with me, I get lonely. It's a bit like being in a dark tunnel and you can't see the light. My daughter is a real tonic (minus the gin). She is almost seven now. We can have a proper conversation with each other; she's a bright little girl.

When my daughter is with me I'm not lonely, loneliness can kill so I tend to go out a lot and relieve the boredom sometimes. When my friend and I had depression we both experienced erratic behaviour. I have my faith in God, which is my foundation to life itself.

Chapter 5

Can You Overcome Depression?

Yes you can by following these guidelines:

1) Don't isolate yourself as this will make you feel worse.

2) Mix with friends that show sympathy and understanding.

3) Talk to someone you can trust, preferably a close friend.

4) Speak with your doctor as they are very understanding.

5) Remember to take your medication as this will make you better.

6) Exercise helps elevate your mood and lifts the spirits.

7) Don't bottle up feelings, talk to someone like a doctor or friend.

8) Don't overdo the housework as this will tire you out physically.

9) Take time out doing enjoyable things for yourself, me time.

10) Don't spend too much money as this can burn a hole in the pocket.

11) Live a simple life not a complicated one.

12) Life today can be challenging, with problem after problem, day after day. Many people do not know the answers to their problems. However whatever problem you have, there is an answer, prayer, it can add focus and meaning to your life. Believe me when you are at your lowest in life, praying to our heavenly father can ease the pain and suffering that you face.

Keep these twelve points in mind as you will find these useful to you. Keep these points close to your mind and heart, meditate upon them. You will start to feel better inside if you follow the recipe for success. Following the recipe for success isn't easy to start with. It takes lots of practise and with time it will get easier, the pill popping gets easier.

Remember depression is a mental illness not a physical one, although when I get really tired I feel like I've had the stuffing knocked out of me. To be honest you get good days and bad days. For me the bad days out-weighed the good days.

Your medication is your lifeline, your tonic, you DO need them to remain fit and healthy. You also need to watch what you eat. I try to eat three healthy meals a day, but I'm afraid to say, I'm still snacking on crisps and some chocolate, I can't resist. I'll never lose weight at this rate. Any way I'll not give up. I'll try to eat more fruit and vegetables as this will help me gradually lose weight.

I have found that many people who suffer from depression have found hope in the bibles' promise: "No resident will say I am sick", taken from Isaiah 33v24. Do you know how I know it's true, that's because God is perfect, he can't lie. I have found the bible a strengthening aid to my recovery. Belief in God is an anchor for the soul. So continue like I said before, take your medication, eat well, sleep well, as this can aid your recovery.

I'm three quarters of the way through writing this book and most of you out there are starting to understand what Bipolar is now and what it's like for the people who suffer, to look at the inside of the mind of the sufferer it's very intense. The mind is a very powerful tool. If not used in the correct way it can be disastrous to the sufferer.

Many people with Bipolar or manic depression have low self-esteem of themselves, they think they are useless in every way. Some people feel like curling up in a ball and dying, the pressure of depression can be so intense at times. These feelings can cause a person to have thoughts of suicide. Believe me, talking from personal experience, this is not the answer. For a start think about your loved ones who you will leave behind, and the utter turmoil that your family would be in. Your family would start blaming themselves for what you've done. Your family would never forgive themselves if you did take your own life. This isn't the answer to your problems.

There are many organizations out there that can help people like me and you when we are distraught or down trodden.

I attend a drop in centre near to where I live. This is for the mentally ill and it's based in Leicestershire. I find this very beneficial to my well-being, since I've been attending this group I have had less trips to the hospital. You can find a Mind group either on the internet or in your local library. It's well worth attending, you can benefit from this scheme. There is always some one on hand when you need help. You can make new friends.

Speaking from personal experience my friend conquered her illness, I'm still battling on with mine. Depression in general isn't easy to cope with, however some times you just have to learn to live with it. You need to try to conquer your illness like my friend did.

Life is so precious to me, like gold, gold is a very precious metal, it glistens in the sunlight. Like I said before my friend overcame so much after such a long time. She is now in remission. I know that one day I will feel just like her, in control again.

When I am well I have lots of energy, a bit like a super woman, however when I'm on a bad day I have no energy, or I can't be in a bothered mood, which I can't get out of. Every thing seems like such an effort. I do try to keep myself well, though this isn't easy.

However my friends' journey inspires me to carry on despite everything. I am trying to follow in her footsteps by being positive every day. I thought I was doing fine up until the other day, don't ask me why, every thing went wrong. I experienced a manic episode. I remember walking around the CO-OP, I didn't feel well at all. In fact I felt like death warmed up. It was so bad I thought I was going to fall to the floor. I was so famished; my whole body went numb with pain. Apparently I hadn't been eating properly and this is the reason why I wasn't feeling well. I was out with a friend when I had a funny turn; we went out for a cup of tea. After I had drunk the tea I felt a lot better and my strength was reinvigorated. I started to feel normal again. Although I still felt dizzy I decided to stay at a friends' house for the night. I tried to relax but couldn't. After taking medication I fell asleep with my friends' cats after praying for some rest.

The next day I felt relaxed and back to normal. I hope I don't have another manic episode like that anyway. You see manic-depressives have many highs and lows in life. I have experienced many lows in my life.

Since my friends' recovery, she has experienced no highs or lows in her life. She is truly an amazing woman. She could tell a few tales or two or even maybe write a book herself.

Some times some one who is severely depressed may be coerced into having E.C.T or (electro convulsive therapy). I was talked into having this treatment, I was told this would help me, but it didn't, it made me worse. However after having about eight shock treatments, instead of making me better it gave me memory loss.

I know of some one else who had at least twenty shock treatments and it made her irritable and forgetful. E.C.T does work for some people not every one. Having E.C.T made me really poorly I kept going in and out of hospital, it traumatized me. However thanks to time, which is a great healer, I am now doing just fine.

I was doing really well up until October 2006 when I ended up in hospital again. I ended up in a small room, it was claustrophobic. I didn't get out of bed for quite some time. I didn't eat or drink much. I was dehydrated to the point when I thought I was dying.

However there was a turning point in my life when I was moved to a dormitory with people. I relaxed and at ease. I started eating and drinking again. I started washing myself again and drank water to cleanse my digestive system.

In order to pass time by quickly I planted some Japanese onions in the hospital allotment. I also did a little knitting. Soon it was time for ward round in the hospital. I was allowed to go home for the day, to see how I would cope in the real world. It was a bit nerve racking for a start, however I soon got into the swing of things. The following week I was allowed to go home for a weeks leave, it went really well. I hoped the week after I would be discharged and to my surprise I was. Since being released from hospital I have been more positive on my outlook on life. This is both me and my friends' story, anyway. Now to relate another friends' story who suffers from Bipolar, this time a lady who really inspires me.

Chapter 6

Anne's Experience

I wish to relate another experience of another friend who suffers from Bipolar. Before being diagnosed she was a happy go lucky sort of gal. She was born and bred in Leicestershire in 1944. She has also been in and out of hospital.

My friend was persuaded into having E.C.T (electro convulsive therapy). She had quite a few treatments, it's a wonder her head didn't explode, it didn't do her much good. My friend got very irritable, moody and forgetful. My friend had more E.C.T treatment.

She was transferred to a day hospital where she had more E.C.T. After a while she started to feel better so she was allowed to go home. She went on a train to meet her mum who was at the station to greet her daughter.

However her recovery didn't last long. It wasn't before long my friend became ill again. She was once more taken to hospital. She had more E.C.T and felt worse after each treatment. Like myself, she kept forgetting things. During her illness she has had many highs and lows in her life. My friend has suffered from depression for about 20yrs.

My friend has never married nor had any children of her own. She is a lovely lady, at a good age. However her depression has been one of the most difficult things for her to cope with. She is still coping now but is finding that the illness is wearing her down slightly. She is one of the bravest ladies I know, and I'm sure given time she will start to bloom and flourish like the lady she is within.

At the moment my friend is on six tablets a day and her health has improved, although she still has highs and lows.

The thing with Bipolar is you can't just wipe it away like a cold, you're stuck with it, there is no known cure at the moment. Thinking positive can help with mood swings. Although my friend is very shy, she is very kind and thoughtful. Although she suffers from Bipolar, she also suffers from arthritis, which can be very painful at times.

Even though my friend is shy she is full of charisma and charm. Although she still suffers from depression she is still hanging on in there. Like I've said before she's at a good age. Although she still suffers she is much to be admired. My friend has suffered a lot during her lifetime but she is still an example of courage. This is my friends' story.

Chapter 7

Dorothys' Experience

We have just been discussing ways with which to combat depression. We are going to now look at another true-life example. The other lady suffering from Bipolar is about 50yrs old. She was born and bred in Airdrie. She has suffered from Bipolar Disorder for at least 35yrs of her life. She was born in 1957 in a town called Lennox in Scotland.

So this young ladys' story begins when she was really well in herself, in the picture of health, unlike my other friend from Airdrie, she became ill like a bolt of lightening, very poorly indeed. She too was hospitalised. Anyway these too ladies were in the hospital at the same time and became close friends. They both experienced mania and each understood what the other was going through, yet one of the ladies mentioned before had a bizarre experience with a church. She was getting deeper and deeper into it, in fact she felt that she had been brain washed.

Before this lady got poorly she was holding down a full-time job teaching in a school. She is a very intelligent woman who has so many good qualities about her. You could say that her life was almost perfect.

However when she got sick, she became very unstable and one push could knock her over the edge. This lady was married to a lovely young man. He was so handsome, the pick of the bunch. In fact married life was blissful, however this state of happiness didn't last long for her. Wherever she went her illness seemed to follow her. She was married in America and lived there for a while. However things started to go wrong in the marriage. Like me and Isabel, money was uncontrollably being spent. Dorothy's husband left her and after two years the relationship had ended in a divorce. After the marriage break-up she went to live in Scotland, where she now lives and has lived there ever since. She suffered for quite some time with her illness but is also now well in herself, holding down a full-time job looking after the mentally ill.

It has now been 20yrs since her illness and she is doing really well and is not on any medication, she lives in a cottage in Lennox in Scotland. Her health is now back to tip top condition. She is a highly educated person, respected in the community. Her friends and family think that this lady is a truly amazing woman for what she's been through. She is also an inspiration to me as well. I certainly feel encouraged by her experience and it's helped me not to give up but to carry on regardless. I feel really inspired by this ladies' experience and this makes me feel inspired to carry on. I now have a positive mental attitude to life and so does Dorothy. This is her experience anyway.

Chapter 8

How Is It All Going To End?

Throughout this book we have discussed what Bipolar is (a chemical imbalance in the brain) which is a condition called manic depression. We have also discussed three examples of manic depression, which includes my example.

In chapter three we discussed six steps to aid a sufferer:

1) Recognise you have a problem.

2) Seek medical advice for your well being. Don't let the depression get worse. Keep taking your medication, this is your life-line.

3) Be positive, look at things in a humorous way, see the funny side of life.

4) Put your favourite C.D on and have a good sing, you will start to feel much better.

5) Take your mind off your illness by doing a hobby, something you enjoy doing, as this will elevate your mood.

6) I have found prayer very powerful in aiding your recovery. It enhances your life.

Follow these guidelines and you will feel better within yourself and it can eventually put the balance back into your life. We have learnt to take care of our bodies, to eat plenty of good food and to exercise daily.

In chapter 4 of this book we have learnt how to analyse the symptoms of depression which are:

1) The first symptom is putting on weight to an excess.

2) The second symptom is a poor diet.

3) The third symptom is a lack of poor hygiene.

4) The fourth symptom is a lack of sleep.

I also experienced a poor lack of sleep. I am currently on sleeping tablets, which help me to get a good nights' sleep at night.

Sometimes I still find it difficult to sleep. I also find it difficult to get out of bed in the morning, I still get the urge to sleep in sometimes.

At weekends I still get my daughter to stay with me and that's always a treat for me. She's doing really well at school, especially now she's seven years old, so energetic, so full of life and beans (not Heinz).

In chapter five of this book we learnt how to overcome depression.

The twelve ways were:

1)   Don't isolate yourself from the outside world.

2) Associate with people who will benefit you not those that have down-trodden you.

3) Talk to a sympathetic listener.

4) Contact your doctor to discuss your problems.

5) MEDICATION is a must.

6) Exercise every day.

7) Don't keep your feelings to yourself.

8) Don't over do the house-work.

9) Take time out for yourself.

10) Don't spend too much money as this can burn a hole in your pocket.

11) Live a simple life, don't cram too much in your life or you will over-load yourself and may become ill.

12) Prayer can help you feel better, knowing that God understands your needs. You can conquer depression, although this will take a considerable amount of time, with myself I'm recovering slowly.

Going back to chapter 6 of the book Snappy But Happy we learnt about Anne. She was born in 1944. She was given at least 20 E.C.T treatments which seemed to work for a while but then she became ill again. She felt as though the treatment had damaged her brain, like myself she forgot things. At the moment she is also doing well. She has also suffered a lot during her lifetime but always bounces back. She's a shy sort of person who has both charisma and charm. Although she still suffers at times she is still much to be admired by all.

In chapter 7 of the book we have a story of success to be told. This ladies' name is Dorothy and she was born in 1957 in a town called Lennox in Scotland. Before she became unwell she used to hold down a full-time job as a teacher in a school and she was married too.

She wasn't married for long, she started to experience problems in the marriage and after a long pain-staking two years she was divorced. When Dorothy was in hospital that is where she met Isabel and they became close friends. When Dorothy became well she went to live in a cottage in Lennox town Scotland. Although she suffered from mania, she was never depressed. She has now been well for twenty years and is on no medication. She is highly adored by family and friends. She is also an inspiration to me. I feel really encouraged by her progress.

From the knowledge you have learnt from how a depressed person feels, it will help you understand people who suffer in a new light. Although you have gained access into a persons thinking ability, maybe you too will be able to say, I'm beating Bipolar Disorder.

The rest of the book is devoted to poetry, which I have written during my recovery. I hope you can identify with some of it, and enjoy reading it.

POETRY IN MOTION

The Wind

Standing still as a cool gentle breeze
Collectively cools the nape of my neck
I look ahead of me, searching for tranquillity
Beneath myself and the wind
But it pushes and shoves me into oblivion
So that I'm in despair
Running for my life
As the noises of the wind
Become apparent to me
Suddenly it turns into a whirlwind
Thrashing and crashing to the floor
Anyone or anything in its path
The power behind me blinds me into confusion
I run with all my spirit, to a safe haven, it eventually subsides.

Poetry In Motion

Poetry in motion
There is much devotion
It's a silly old notion
But there's a poet in the making
Is what I'm creating
So forget about the words
It's the body of the poem
That's what makes it so good
So try and remember it as you should.

Child O' Mine

O child o' mine how sweet you are
O child o' mine with soft blonde locks
A young and perfect skin
Is what she's deeply within
She's got a heart of gold so I'm told
Such beauty in perfection
Is a story that is told
My little Lydia is never ever growing old.

<u>Roses</u>

I'm like the red, red rose
So scarlet does it pose
It's so delicate and fine
I'm going to make it mine
The rose is a delightful flower
Its petals make a fine shower
I feel quite sad.

<u>Depression</u>

There was a time when I was down
I wouldn't speak I wouldn't frown
I'd just shuffle along
Like nothing's wrong
But I can't fool anyone
That I'm ok
All I wish that the depression, go away.

<u>Imagine</u>

Imagine never growing old
Imagine turning the hands of time
Imagine never being sick
Imagine getting rid of old Nick
Imagine peace and harmony
Imagine plenty of food
Imagine never dying
But living forever
It's not just a dream
But it's a reality
And it will be seen.

Fruit&Veg

I'm on a strict diet and that is true
Fruit and veg are good for you
Eat 3 lots of fruit and 5 lots of veg
And then you won't be on the edge
Eat apples, pears and bananas too
Strawberries enrich, vitamins too
Eat plenty of carrots, peas and beans
But this isn't as easy as it seems
Sick to your diet and that's a mission
You know before long you'll be in better condition.

Two Hearts

To a young couple it's surely bliss
The moment when you steal a kiss
Her heart is touched so tenderly
His heart melts so fast
Oh surely it will last
Two hearts that beat as one
Surely it has begun
Maybe he'll sweep her off her feet
With romantic notions still very deep
It makes one want to weep
So sleep well with all my love
Says the husband to his new wife with love.

Sooty

My cat is called Sooty

He's black all over

He's so handsome

He's the pick of the bunch

He's an indoor cat

With so much charm and grace

He's the cutest cat in the human race

His claws are sharp, razor like too

So come and pet him, he loves you too.

The Circus

I can see clowns in the big top
Juggling balls and laughing out loud
Oh what a big crowd
The ringmaster cracks his whip to the floor
The lion jumps out of his cage with a roar
The tightrope walker makes sure of his balance
People laugh and people cheer
As the tightrope walker makes it clear
He's made it to the end
The crowd gives a cheer
As the end of the day draws near.

<u>Creation</u>

When God made man
He had a plan
For man and beast to live in peace
But that went wrong
After Eve came along
And ruined it for all
So all men fall into sin
And that's where we begin
So don't you worry and don't you fret
It's not all over yet
Jesus gave his life for you and me
So we could be set free.

Just Friends

Me and my girl are just friends
Our friendship never ends
I make her laugh
I make her squeal
I make her cry
It's so unreal
She's a real tonic
As you may wonder
It's me and my girl
So don't steal my thunder.

Robin Red Breast

As I look out of the window
I see a fair robin looking for food
He has a red chest
So plump and fair
He's ever so rare
Poor old robin couldn't find a mate
He's stuck on his own
I can't contemplate what he'll do
He'll either fly away or make it through the winter.

<u>Butterflies</u>

Butterflies, butterflies everywhere you go
Wherever you go they are there
Blue ones, yellow ones, pink and red
Come and see them before they fly
High in the sky
I wonder why?

Lucy

I have a friend
She's very special to me
She's the kindest lady I know
I love to help her out you know
She's so sweet and gentle
And lovely she is too
So come and meet her
It's Lucy James you know.

Moods

When I'm in the mood
I just love to eat food
From burgers and mash to jacket spud
Followed by chicken curry in a hurry
When I'm in a bad way I pray
This helps my mood swings
It elevates my soul
That my friend is my goal.

Mirror

As I gaze up in my mirror
I see myself as never before
A young woman
With so much charm and grace
I'm the luckiest gal in the human race
So much beauty within my inner self
There's no doubt her beauty is skin deep.

Daffodil

The daffodil o what a flower
It's been picked this very hour
I love daffs because they are yellow
They glisten in the sunshine
I'm going to make them mellow.

Trees

I see trees with their leaves
Blown to the ground
They are red, green and brown
Trees have aged dramatically
They are refreshing as the leaves fall to the floor
And then they are no more.

__Snowflakes__

I see the crispness of the snow

It glitters like a star

It's lovely and white

On a clear night

Each flake is unique

As we speak

It is true there are snowflakes all around you.

<u>Television</u>

I don't tend to watch the box
There's nothing I can watch
It's all bad stuff you know
Violence or sex is the up town beat
Of todays society so to speak
The standards of tv have dropped
They are to be stopped
There's not a lot I can watch
But I love the nature progs.

Dolphins

I look around me I can see them
Swimming jumping through hoops
Making children laugh as they splash the water on the crowd
This is aloud
They duck and dive
They also thrive
Looking and chuckling at the crew
To swim with a dolphin that would be ever so cool
Dolphins are intelligent just like us
So come and see them
Make a fuss and watch them cackle
They're a feisty bunch but hard to tackle
So the moral of the story may be
To swim with a dolphin for free.

Life

For longevity in your life
Make sure you are free from strife
All your worries should be put aside
As you worship God in your stride
It's not an easy ride
So abide by the rules
You are no mere fools
But what you have is deep inside
You've still got your pride.

<u>The Bed</u>

Oh how I do love my bed
I'm such a sleepy head
If I could stop in bed all day
I'd choose to do this without delay
The bed is so comfy, snugly and warm
I'd sooner stay in bed where it's warm.

Time

Time doesn't stand

It is grand

The wrist of my own hand

As I gaze at the clock

All I hear is tick-tock tick-tock tick-tock

Time goes by

I wonder why?

Why don't you stand still if you will

Time doesn't stand still for any one.

<u>Washing</u>

Washing, washing everyday

Pegged on the line and there to stay

A strong gust of wind knocks the washing off the line

It gets all muddy on the ground

So up it's picked and washed again

I hope it doesn't rain again.

The Body

All of us have one and that is true
Some don't work properly, some do
But to this effect may you be well
This is as far as I can tell
The body is well made
And that's for sure
The creator made us to endure.

Music

I'm not tone deaf
If that's what you think
My music may be loud
Oh I'm ever so proud
Music is my potion
So much devotion
Music uplifts my soul
It is my role
So whatever you think
I'm in tune with the beat.

Chocolate

How lovely you are so brown and smooth

It oozes drips off my tongue

I hope it's not going to be too long

Before I can taste it again

My favourite is Mars

It helps you work rest and play

Although a Milky Way is said to be fair play

Chocolate is good

Eat it we should

It's soothing to the soul

So I'm told

So lo and behold, the chocolate treat

That we're meant to eat

It's delicious and good, so eat it we should.

Peace

I have inner peace and inner calm

I shall do you no harm

It's just peace that I pursue

To help me get to know the real you

But my love is no more

I have to be sure

I can still reach him with a kiss

Oh that is what I surely miss

It's peace from above

It surely was love.

Rain

Rain is good for the garden
Rain is good for the soil
In fact rain is good for us
It clears the air
Makes it crisp and new
Rain makes the flowers bloom
Especially in the month of June
We shouldn't huff or puff
If rain comes our way
Be grateful that it's here and here to stay.

The Mind

The mind is a powerful tool

It can aid and destroy

Is what I employ

So many choices we have to make

In our lives so to speak

The mind absorbs just like a sponge

So if you want to take the plunge

It's a funny old thing the mind that's true

So take my advice, don't put yourself to blame

It's the name of the game.

Jembe

I used to play the African drum
Now I'm a full-time mum
I still play from time to time
It's catchy and that is true
So come and play with me too
We'll get you rocking to the beat
And even dancing in the street
So come and learn the Jembe like me
And then you yourself will be free.

Reflections

I peer deeply into the mirror
Looking for dimples or wrinkles
In desperation I apply the cream
This is no mere dream
It's simply old age.

Horses

I love to see the horses run
It looks to me like a lot of fun
The steed is ready
And that's a must
You have to depend on trust
Horses are a bit like us
Independent and intelligent creatures
Is what it features
So when I see the horse in its stride
I'd often think I'd like a ride.

Poet

She's a poet in the making
Is what I'm creating
Sound in body and sound in mind
To this you'll find
Poetically inclined
Oh she is a rare kind
In a perfect state of mind.

Telephone

The ringing tone of a telephone
Is much to be inspired and admired
It's wired for sound when I'm around
It's my lifeline to the world
Outside of these four walls
I'm as young as I feel
It's so unreal
The telephone brings me joy
I make a few calls per day
And that keeps me at bay for today.

<u>Elephants</u>

Elephants waddle to and fro
Elephants are good you know
They swish their tails and fill their trunks
They move about from side to side
If you ask them nicely they will give you a ride.

<u>Camels</u>

Camels, camels everywhere
They have got two humps
So I don't care
It's a bumpy ride on a camel that's true
It's a bumpy ride, for me and you.

Dolly

My doll is perfect to a T
She's young and beautiful
Just like me
She wears her hair
Just right you know
Dressed to impress I am
She's my dolly my dolly Ann.

<u>Suffering</u>

There are many in the world
That are in despair
Suffering turmoil in their lives
God tells us that sickness and death will soon be long gone
We look forward to the time when that day arrives
All wickedness will soon be long gone
And then we won't go wrong
Only the good will stay
And to carry on living they may
So take action without delay
If you want to remain in Gods way.

<u>Bipolar</u>

I used to feel really sad
But now I'm happy I'm not just mad
I was really low so down and distraught
I must remember to forget that thought
I feel as good as I can be
I'm thankful that I'm alive you see
Being manic isn't all that bad
I try to cope the best way I can
It's all about helping the one you love
Seek Godly wisdom from above.

Water

Water is vital for life
The body needs it every day
Water cleanses the soul
That my friend is its role
Drink it we should
As often as we can
Water is a healing tool
It refreshes and renews
It's a source from up above
We should learn to live and share
With this product that is so rare.

The New World

The new world will be full of joy
Peace and harmony will employ
No one to make you tremble with fear
In fact all earths' woes will disappear
To that end may we have faith that's strong
So that we may never go wrong
The worlds' in a mess there's no doubt
Only Gods' kingdom that can put it right
So please brothers and sisters don't give up the fight
It's a struggle sometimes to run the race
So many temptations we have to face
So please bear in mind we are not on our own
So try not to worry about what to do
Jehovah himself will pull you through.

About The Author

My name is Lorna Murby and I'm a real down to earth lass. I live in Coalville, Leicestershire. I have three sisters and one half brother, their names are Sallyanne, Rebecca and Paula, my brothers' name is Peter.

Paula has two children called Kal and Jacey. Rebecca has a little boy called Jacob. I have a little girl called Lydia who is a sweet heart, the apple of my eye. My hobbies are: knitting, crochet, crossword competitions, listening to music. I like some pop and some classical. My favourite two instruments are: the harp and the saxophone.

I also like doing girlie things like shopping for make up and clothes. I have enjoyed writing this book immensely. I hope readers out there feel inspired by my book and want to read it over and over again. I am confident that this book will be the winner that it is. This book is not just for the sufferer, but for every one else in the world.